Subscribe to the Newsletter!

Your email address
Subscribe

Table of Contents

Amazing Hot Chocolate Recipes

ZZZZZZZZZZZZZZZZZZZZZZZZZZZZZZZZZZZZZZZZZZZZZZZZZZ
ZZZZZZZZZ

Chapter I - Healthy

ZZZZZZZZZZZZZZZZZZZZZZZZZZZZZZZZZZZZZZZZZZZZ
ZZZZZZZZZZZ

1) Raspberry Ruffle Hot Chocolate

Chocolate and fruit complement each other brilliantly, especially raspberries and milk delicious chocolate!

Makes: 2

Preparation Time: 10mins

Component Checklist:

1/2 cup sugar

1/4 cup chilly water

12 ounces fresh raspberries 1 1/2 mugs whole milk

1/4 mug cacao powder (bitter) 2 tbsps confectioner' s sugar

Guidelines:

Add the sugar, water, and raspberries to a saucepan as well as bring to steam. Take off the warmth and also press through a screen to leave a smooth puree. In a clean saucepan, cozy the milk, taking treatment not to steam. Add the

cocoa powder, confectioner' s sugar, and also set apart puree.
3. Serve promptly!

2)   Pumpkin Spice White Hot Chocolate

The taste of fall in a cup! Put your feet up in front of a roaring fire and also sip on this spicy wonderful reward.
Makes:3 - 4
Preparation Time: 20mins
Component Checklist:
1 mug white choc chips

Guidelines:

2 cups skim milk 1 cup whipping cream
1/2 teaspoons vanilla significance
1/2 teaspoons pumpkin seasoning Whip cream (for covering) Pumpkin
seasoning (for covering)

1. Include the choc chips to a dish and set aside.
2. Inasmallsaucepanwarmthemilk, andcreamovermedium warm. Simmer yet
do not steam.
3. Put the hot milk mixture over the choc chips and stir well till thawed as
well as smooth.
4. Include the vanilla as well as flavor. Mix well.
5. Pour into mugs and leading with whip lotion and a cleaning of pumpkin pie
spice.

3) Hot Chocolate Affogato

A favorite reward in Italy, affogato typically sees a shot of espresso put over a scoop of vanilla ice cream. This version swaps coffee for scrumptious homemade hot delicious chocolate.

Makes:6 - 8

Prep Work Time: 7mins

Ingredient List:

2 mugs skim milk

2 tbsps chocolate powder (semisweet) 1 mug choc chips (semisweet)

⅛ teaspoons sea salt

1 pint premium vanilla bean ice cream

Directions:

1. In a tiny saucepan cozy the milk over tool heat. Simmer however do not boil. When the milk starts to quietly bubble at the sides, include the cocoa powder, stylish chops and sea salt. Whisk well until smooth.
2. Into coffee cups or little bowls scoop little rounds of ice cream.
3. Pour over a' shot' of the warm delicious chocolate and serve!

4) Vegan Chai Hot Chocolate

A delightful dairy - free warm chocolate that every person can take pleasure in, also those following a vegan diet regimen!

Makes: 2

Prep Work Time: 10mins

Component Checklist:

2 cups vanilla sweetened almond milk 2 tbsps chocolate powder

1 tablespoon chai spice

Directions:

1. Include all ingredients to a pan as well as bring to steam. Warmth, while mixing

till the cocoa and spice have liquified.

2. Decline the heat as well as bring to a simmer. Prepare for 4 - 6 minutes, put right into mugs as well as offer!

5) Hot Chocolate with Sea Salt Whip Cream

Who doesn' t love mixing salty and also wonderful tastes!? This delicious salt spiked whip lotion aids stabilize the luscious sweet taste of thick hot delicious chocolate.

Makes: 1
Preparation Time: 15mins
Component List: Whip lotion:
1 tablespoon granulated sugar 1 mug whipping cream
3tablespoons chocolate powder
3/4 teaspoons sea salt

Warm chocolate:
4ounces dark baking chocolate
1 ounce semisweet cooking delicious chocolate
3/4 mug milk
3 tsps honey

Instructions:

1. In an electric mixer, whip up the sugar as well as lotion, until you have very soft tops.
2. Add the salt and also cocoa powder as well as whisk delicately, until included. Set aside.
3. Utilizing a double central heating boiler, melt the two sorts of chocolate and stir well. Include the milk as well as honey to the dissolved delicious chocolate as well as mix well. Continue to heat till very warm.
4. Put into mugs and top with a generous glob of the sea salt whip lotion.
5. Serve!

6) Unicorn Hot Chocolate

This lovely purple white warm delicious chocolate is ensured to bring a little magic to your day!

Makes: 2

Preparation Time: 10mins

Ingredient Listing:

4 mugs entire milk

1 tsp vanilla significance

8 ounces white chocolate (chopped)

2 tablespoons pink fining sand sugar 2 tbsps blue sanding sugar Whip lotion (for covering)

Rainbow hundreds and thousands (for topping)

Instructions:

1. Add the milk, vanilla essence and white chocolate to a pan over reduced -

tool heat. Stir at intervals up until thawed as well as smooth.

2. Add the sugars as well as stir until dissolved.

3. Pour into cups as well as top with whip cream as well as a dropping of thousands as well as hundreds.

4. Offer!

7) Lavender Hot Chocolate

To appreciate this flower fancy in the house, begin by making lavender instilled milk.

Makes: 4
Prep Work Time: 15mins
Component Checklist:
4 cups milk
1 tablespoon dried out lavender
3/4 mug hot delicious chocolate mix
1/2 teaspoons vanilla significance

Instructions:

1. In a small pan warm the milk over med heat.Toss in the dried lavender and offer a simmer.
2. Remove the warm and reserve for 5 - 7 mins.
3. Return to the heat and add in the hot delicious chocolate mix. Whisk well and also remove the warm once more.
4. Mix with the vanilla significance. Stress into 4 mugs and serve!

8) Tres Leches Coco Cocoa

Tres leches suggests 3 milks, this thick, decadent beverage incorporates condensed milk, coconut milk and also skim milk.

Makes:3 - 4

Preparation Time: 10mins

Component Checklist:

2 cups skim milk

14 ounces light unsweetened coconut milk 7 ounces sweetened condensed milk

2 tbsps cocoa powder (unsweetened)

1/2 teaspoons vanilla significance Whip cream (for covering)

Dry coconut (for covering)

Guidelines:

1. In a saucepan over a low - medium warmth, add the 3 milks and whisk well.

2. Take and simmer the milk treatment not to boil it, or enable it to swelter the frying pan.

3. Add the cocoa powder and whisk well.

4. Take the pan off the warmth as well as mix in the vanilla.

5. Put right into cups as well as top with whip lotion and a scattering of desiccated coconut.

9) Lemongrass and Lime Zest White Hot Chocolate

The Oriental flavors of aromatic lemongrass and zingy lime zest cut through the velvety richness of the thick white warm delicious chocolate.

Makes: 2

Prep Work Time: 20mins

Active ingredient Checklist:

12 ounces milk

1/2 tsps dried out lavender

1 stalk lemongrass (chopped) 1 lime leaf (torn)

Guidelines:

1/2 tsps fresh lime passion
3 ounces white delicious chocolate (chopped)

4. In a little saucepan warm the milk, lavender, lemongrass, lime leaf as well as enthusiasm over medium warm. Heat up until the blend starts to bubble at the edges.
5. Take off the warmth and also reserve for 15 mins.
6. Stress the milk into a container, throwing out everything left behind. Return the strained milk to the saucepan.
7. Include the chocolate and mix well until it is melted and completely incorporated.
8. Serve quickly.

10) Red Velvet Hot Chocolate

European styled warm delicious chocolate complemented with whip cream and collapsed red velvet cake. A real showstopper!

Makes: 4

Prep Work Time: 5mins

Ingredient List:

3 mugs whole milk

1 1/2 mugs semi sweet choc chips Red food gel

Whip lotion (for covering)

Red velour cake (collapsed, for topping)

Guidelines:

1. In a saucepan over tool heat, include the milk as well as choc chips. Stir well

till thawed and also silky.

2. Add the red food gel, a little at once till you reach your desired shade of red.

3. Pour into cups and also leading with whip lotion and also a dropping of collapsed cake.

11) Milk Chocolate and PB Hot Chocolate

Forget jam; milk delicious chocolate is the utmost companion to smooth and velvety peanut butter!

Makes: 1

Preparation Time: 20mins

Component Checklist:

1/4 mug half and half 1 cup entire milk

1/4 cup milk choc chips

1 tbsp smooth peanut butter

1/4 cup mini mallows

Instructions:

1. Add the compromise as well as milk to a saucepan as well as offer a simmer over low - tool warm.

2. When the mixture starts to steam, add the choc chips.Stir well up until

they have actually melted.

3. Add the peanut butter and also mix again.
4. Put into a mug and also scatter with small mallows.
5. Offer and also delight in.

Chapter II - Non - Alcoholic
ZZZZZZZZZZZZZZZZZZZZZZZZZZZZZZZZZZZZZZZZZZ
ZZZZZZZZZZZ

12) Ginger Spiced Hot Cocoa

Fresh ginger brings zingy flavor to this rich dark delicious chocolate warm chocolate.

Makes: 1

Prep Work Time: 10mins

Ingredient List:

1/4" portion ginger (peeled off, sliced) 8 ounces skim milk

2 tsps granulated sugar

2 tsps cocoa powder (unsweetened) 2 tsps water

⅛ ounces dark delicious chocolate (grated)

Guidelines:

1. In a tiny saucepan warm the ginger as well as milk over a low - med warmth.
Simmer however do not mix as well as steam at periods for 5 minutes.
2. Into a cup, add the sugar and also chocolate powder as well as pour in the water. Mix well to form a paste.
3. Throw out the ginger from the milk.
4. Include the delicious chocolate paste to the milk as well as whisk. When frothy, put into a mug and also serve with a sprinkling of the chocolate shavings.

13) Cardamom - Infused Hot Chocolate

Butter brings a deep splendor that pairs with the fragrant cardamom flavor perfectly.

Makes: 1

Preparation Time: 15mins

Ingredient List:

1 cup whole milk

3 cardamom sheathings (crushed)

2 tablespoons chopped dark delicious chocolate 1 teaspoon saltless butter

1/2 teaspoons vanilla essence

Guidelines:

1. In a saucepan over a reduced - tool heat, cozy the milk as well as cardamom.
Give a simmer for 8 - 10 mins.
2. In a separate saucepan on a low - tool heat, melt with each other the delicious chocolate as well as butter.
3. Strain the hot milk into a jug, throwing out the cardamom. Instantly, pour the milk into the melted chocolate, while stirring continually. Add the vanilla, mix well and also offer!

14) 2 - Ingredient Hot Chocolate

Yes, that's appropriate! An indulgent and also pleasantly thick powder complimentary warm chocolate made with simply 2 active ingredients; hazelnut chocolate spread and also milk.

Makes: 1

Prep Work Time: 5mins

Active **Ingredient List:**

1cup semi skim milk

2tablespoons hazelnut chocolate spread

Directions:

1. In a tiny pan over tool - high warmth, prepare the milk up until

steaming.

2. Include the hazelnut chocolate spread as well as mix well up until it has completely included into the milk.
3. Offer immediately!

15) Festive Peppermint Hot Chocolate

Absolutely nothing makes us really feel extra joyful than a cozy mug of pepperminty warm chocolate.

Makes: 4

Preparation Time: 10mins

Component Listing:

1 1/4 mugs choc chips (semisweet) 2 mugs heavy cream

2 mugs semi skim milk

1/2 tsps vanilla significance

1/2 tsps pepper mint essence

Guidelines:

1. Add the choc chips to a heatproof bowl and reserved.
2. In a small saucepan warm the lotion and milk over medium warmth. Simmer however do not boil and also stir at periods.
3. When warm, put the mix over the delicious chocolate.
4. Include the significances as well as whisk well until smooth.
5. Put into cups and also serve!

16) Aztec Dark Cinnamon Cocoa

The Aztecs were in fact among the initial to find delicious chocolate as well as considered it to be a gift from the Gods, and even used cacao beans as a type of currency. They promptly discovered that cacao can be made use of to make a tasty drink and also spiced it with cinnamon.

Makes: 4

Preparation Time: 5mins

Active **Ingredient List:**

6cups whole milk

10 ounces dark delicious chocolate (cut)

1/4 tsps ground cinnamon

Instructions:

1. In a little pan over a reduced - medium warm, cozy together the milk and also sliced delicious chocolate. Stir well until totally thawed and also integrated.
2. Spray in the cinnamon and stir once more.

3. Pour right into mugs and also offer!

17) Chile Spice Hot Chocolate

Some like it hot! Ancho chile powder brings the warm to this delicious warming mug of cocoa.

Makes: 4

Prep Work Time: 10mins

Active ingredient Checklist:

4cups semi skim milk

1/2 cup chocolate powder (bitter)

1/2 mug granulated sugar

1/4 teaspoons cinnamon

1/2 teaspoons ancho chile powder Sea salt flakes

Marshmallows (for topping)

Guidelines:

In a pan over medium warm, add the milk, cocoa, granulated sugar, cinnamon, ancho chile powder and a pinch of sea salt flakes. Turn the heat down to a simmer as well as cook for 5 - 6 mins.

2. Pour into cups, leading with marshmallows and offer!

18) Brownie Batter Chocolate

If you' re the individual that enjoys to lick the dish when making brownies, then this is the warm delicious chocolate for you! Recreate that delicious taste by using a boxed brownie mix.

Makes:8 - 12

Preparation Time: 10mins

Active **Ingredient List:**

2/3 cup heavy cream

1/4 mug light corn syrup

1/2 mug light brownish sugar

1/4 mug boxed brownie mix

Instructions:

1 cup choc chips (semisweet) 1 tsp vanilla essence
8 mugs milk

1. Over tool warm, integrate the very first 4 components as well as fifty percent of the choc chips in a small pan. Warmth till thawed and also smooth. Stir with the staying choc chips until integrated. Reserve.
2. In a different pan warm the milk. Mix the brownie mixture right into the heated milk and serve!

19)   Cheesecake Hot Chocolate

This yummy beverage integrates our 2 preferred deals with; cheesecake as well as cacao!

Makes: 2

Preparation Time: 10mins

Active Ingredient Listing:

1cup entire milk

2ounces full fat cream cheese (cut into 16 items, area temperature)

1/4 tsps vanilla significance

2 ounces sliced white delicious chocolate

Directions:

Whip lotion (for covering)
Crumbed graham biscuits (for covering)

1. In a saucepan over tool heat, warm the milk yet do not boil.
2. Refuse the warmth as well as blend in the cream cheese and also vanilla.
3. Include the chocolate as well as blend up until completely melted and integrated.
4. Pour right into mugs as well as top with whip lotion as well as a sprinkling of graham cracker crumbs.
5. Offer immediately!

20)   Candy Cane White Hot Chocolate

This luscious sweet white hot delicious chocolate is integrated smashed sweet canes and heated in a sluggish cooker. Specifically terrific if you' re getting ready for a group.

Makes:8 - 10

Preparation Time: 1hour 30mins

Active Ingredient List:

8 cups milk

8 ounces white baking chocolate (sliced small)

1/2 mug sweet canes (smashed)

1/2 teaspoons vanilla essence

Instructions:

Whip lotion (for covering) Sweet canes (for offering)

1. Into your slow-moving cooker, add the milk, delicious chocolate, sweet walking canes and vanilla essence.
2. Cover with a lid as well as on a high warm, cook for 90 minutes, mixing ever before quarter of an hour.
3. Serve in cups with a swirl of whip cream as well as a candy walking cane stirrer.

Chapter III - Alcoholic

ZZZZZZZZZZZZZZZZZZZZZZZZZZZZZZZZZZZZZZZZZZZZZZZZZZZ
ZZZZZZZZZ

21) Vanilla Latte Hot Chocolate

Coffee liqueur brings an added saucy caffeine kick to this vanilla cappucino flavored warm chocolate.

Makes: 1

Preparation Time: 20mins

Ingredient List:

1 1/2 ounces coffee liqueur

1/2 cup prepared instant vanilla latte mix

1/2 cup hot delicious chocolate

Instructions:

1. Add all components to a huge mug as well as mix well.
2. Serve quickly!

Black Cherry Bourbon Hot Chocolate

A completely expanded - up warm chocolate; warming, as well as indulgent.

Makes: 2

Preparation Time: 10mins

Ingredient Listing:

1 1/2 mugs entire milk

5 tbsps double chocolate hot chocolate mix 2 ounces black cherry flavor bourbon

Whipped cream Delicious chocolate shavings

Directions:

1. Using a small pan, warmth the milk together with the dual chocolate warm delicious chocolate mix on tool to high warm. Warmth carefully till the milk is steaming as opposed to steaming.

2. Mix to combine the milk with the mix.

3. Add 1 ounce of flavor bourbon per cup. Put the warm chocolate evenly between the cups as well as leading with lashings of whip cream and chocolate shavings.

23) Triple Irish Hot Chocolate

This boozy delicious chocolate packs a major punch with stout, Irish lotion and also whiskey! Certainly one for the grown-ups.

Makes: 4

Preparation Time: 20mins

Component Checklist:

12 ounces Irish stout beer

1/4 cup chocolate powder 1 tablespoon sugar Pinch sea salt

3cups milk

4ounces milk choc chips

4 ounces bittersweet choc chips 4 ounces Irish cream liqueur

4 ounces bourbon

Guidelines:

1. Include the stout to a pan and chef up until the fluid has actually lowered to half a mug. Place to one side.

2. In a different saucepan, add the next 6 active ingredients. Heat till the delicious chocolate milk and also the mixture is heated up with. Whisky

gently.

3. Add in the collection - aside stout, Irish cream as well as whiskey.Use a hand blender to blend up the mix.

4. Pour right into mugs and serve straight away!

24) Boozy Orange Hot Chocolate

Delicious chocolate as well as orange are a timeless combination; shake it up with a splash of orange liqueur and also rum.

Makes: 4

Preparation Time: 7mins

Ingredient Listing:

1/4 mug cacao powder 1 tbsp sugar Pinch sea salt

3cups entire milk

4ounces milk choc chips

4 ounces bittersweet choc chips 3 ounces orange liqueur

4 ounces rum

Whip lotion (for topping)

Instructions:

Candied orange peel (for topping)

1. Add the initial 6 active ingredients to a pan over tool warm. Mix while home heating, till the delicious chocolate melts as well as the blend, is silky.
2. Include the liqueur and rum, stir well.
3. Pour right into cups as well as leading with a charitable dollop of whip cream and also item of candied peel.

25)   Tipsy Double Hazelnut Hot Chocolate

Hazelnut chocolate spread and also hazelnut liqueur bring a lot of nutty flavor.

Makes:2 - 4

Prep Work Time: 10mins

Ingredient Checklist:

1 mug milk

1/4 cup + 2 tablespoons hazelnut delicious chocolate spread 2 tbsps heavy cream

3 tablespoons hazelnut liqueur 2 tbsps brandy

Directions:

1. Include the milk, hazelnut chocolate spread, and heavy cream to a pan over medium heat. Stir as well as cook up until the spread has actually thawed down and completely

integrated.

2. Transform the warmth down reduced and add the alcohols. Stir and warmth up until the drink is very warm however not steaming.

3. Put into mugs and also offer!

26) Butterscotch Whiskey Hot Chocolate

A rich, chocolatey flavour, with a caramel flavour scotch kick.
Makes: 2
Prep Work Time: 10mins
Active ingredients
1/3 cup chilly water
2 tablespoons unsweetened cacao powder 1 tablespoon sugar
2/ 3 cup semi - wonderful choc chips 2 cups milk
1/4 cup butterscotch flavour whiskey Whip cream

Sugar Sauce:
4 tbsps (1/2 stick) salted butter
1/2 mug light brown sugar

1/4 cup heavy cream
2 tablespoons butterscotch scotch

Guidelines:

1. Make the caramel sauce. Using a small pan, over medium heat, include the salty butter, brownish sugar and cream. Offer a swift boil as well as allow to simmer for 60 seconds. Remove the pan from the heat as well as mixing, include the 2 tbsps of scotch. Ready to one side.
2. In a medium pan, integrate the water, chocolate powder, and sugar as well as bring to a mild simmer. Include the chocolate chips as well as whole milk, and while mixing, warm till the chips have actually melted, as well as the fluid is just hot.
3. Gather the butterscotch scotch as well as stir to incorporate.
4. Pour the warm delicious chocolate right into 2 mugs and also leading with a dashboard of whip cream and a sugar sauce.

27) Spiked Coffee Chocolate

Milk instilled with fresh coffee beans brings an additional dimension of coffee taste.

Makes: 2

Prep Work Time: 1hour 10mins

Active ingredient Checklist:

1/2 cup whole milk

1/2 cup heavy cream

1/4 cup coffee beans

2 ounces 60 % semisweet delicious chocolate

Directions:

2 tablespoons coffee liqueur

1. Include the lotion, milk and coffee beans into a pan over tool warm. Remove the warmth and also set aside to steep, protected, for an hour.
2. Stress the mix right into a container as well as throw out the coffee beans.
3. Return the mix to the saucepan and also remind simmer. Add the delicious chocolate as well as heat up until melted as well as included.
4. Take off the warm as well as stir in the liqueur.
5. Pour into mugs and also serve!

Cookies n Crème Minty Hot Chocolate

Cookies, marshmallows, chocolate and minty vodka all in one glass . What more could anyone possibly want?

Makes: 1

Preparation Time: 5mins

Ingredient List:

- 1 ounce mint flavor vodka
- 1 cup white hot chocolate (cooled
-) 3 mint cookies
- 3 mini marshmallows (to serve)
- Mint cookie (to serve)

ZZZZZZZZZZZZZZZZZZZZZZZZZZZZZZZZZZZZZZZZZZZZ
ZZZZZZZZZZZ

Instructions:

1 . To a food, blender add the vodka, white hot chocolate and cookies . Blitz until smooth . Transfer to a small pan and gently heat until steaming but not boiling .

2 . Pour the hot chocolate into a heatproof glass and garnish with mini marshmallows and a mint cookie .

29) Skinny Amaretto Hot Chocolate

Yes, you really can still enjoy a cup of boozy hot chocolate and watch your waistline at the same time .

Makes: 1 - 2

Preparation Time: 5mins

Ingredient List:

- 2 cups almond milk
- 5 teaspoons good quality cocoa powder
- ⅛ - ¼ teaspoons maple
- syrup 1 ounce amaretto

Instructions:

1 . Add all ingredients to a small saucepan over medium - high heat .

2 . Use a whisk to stir the mixture until totally combined and heated through .

3 . Serve straight away !

30) Double Chocolate Maple Cocoa

Cocoa powder and dark chocolate liqueur make for a seriously intense chocolate flavor .

Makes: 1

Preparation Time: 5mins

Ingredient List:

- 2 tablespoons sugar
- 1 tablespoon unsweetened cocoa powder 1 cup whole milk
- Pinch sea salt
- 1 ounce bourbon
- 1 ounce dark chocolate liqueur

ZZZZZZZZZZZZZZZZZZZZZZZZZZZZZZZZZZZZZZZZZZZZ
Instructions ZZZZZZZZZZZ
:

1 . Add the first 4 ingredients in a small saucepan over medium heat
.
Whisk continuously until the mixture is hot but take care not to boil .
2 . Pour into a mug and add the bourbon and liqueur . Stir gently
and serve !

31) Red Wine Hot Chocolate

Red wine makes this hot chocolate extra rich and intense . The perfect after dinner tipple .

Makes:3 - 6
Preparation Time: 5mins
Ingredient List:

- ⅓ cup dark chocolate (chopped)
- 1½ cups skim milk
- 1 cup cabernet red wine

ZZZZZZZZZZZZZZZZZZZZZZZZZZZZZZZZZZZZZZZZZZZZ
Instructions ZZZZZZZZZZZZ
:

1 . Add the choc chips and milk to a saucepan on a medium heat .
2 . Cook until the chocolate has melted and the mixture is silky .

3 . Pour in the cabernet, stir and continue to heat until the mixture is very warm .

4 . Pour into mugs and serve !

32) Double Drunken Pumpkin White Hot Chocolate

This spiked white hot chocolate is practically a pumpkin pie in a mug . With pumpkin puree, pumpkin spice and a healthy dose of bourbon we can ' t think of a better way to celebrate the festive season .

Makes:2

Preparation Time: 10mins

Ingredient List:

- ½ cup white chocolate (chopped) 2½ cups skim milk (divided)
- ¼ cup pumpkin puree
- ¼ teaspoons pumpkin pie spice
- ½ ounce Bourbon

ZZZZZZZZZZZZZZZZZZZZZZZZZZZZZZZZZZZZZZZZZZZZZZZ

Instructions ZZZZZZZZZZZ

:

1 . Melt together the chocolate and half a cup of milk in a saucepan over low - med heat .

2 . Pour in the rest of the milk and the pumpkin puree and spice . Stir well until incorporated and take off the heat .

3 . Pour a little of the hot chocolate into two mugs . Add a ¼ ounce of bourbon to each and then top both with more hot chocolate . Stir gently with a long spoon and serve !

33) Pecan Pie Hot Chocolate with Bourbon

When you want a little me time, take five and settle down with this pecan infused hot chocolate drink .

Makes: 1

Preparation Time: 5mins

Ingredient List:

- 1 cup hot chocolate (cooled
-) 1 ounce bourbon
- 5 pecans
- 2 teaspoons pecan pie
- filling Whip cream

Pecans (for serving)
Pecan pie filling (for serving)

ZZZZZZZZZZZZZZZZZZZZZZZZZZZZZZZZZZZZZZZZZZZZZZZ
ZZZZZZZZZZZ

Instructions
:

1 . Using a food blender, combine the cooled chocolate along with the
bourbon, pecans, and pie filling . Blitz until smooth and then in a small
saucepan, heat the mixture .

2 . Pour the hot chocolate into a tall mug and garnish with whip cream,
pecans, and pie filling .

34) Gin and Lime White Hot Chocolate

Fresh, zesty lime helps to bring out the crisp botanical flavor of the gin .

Makes: 1

Preparation Time: 5mins

Ingredient List:

- 3½ ounces white chocolate (chopped)
- ½ cup warm
- water 1¾ tablespoons gin
- Whip cream (for topping
-) Freshly grated zest of a lime

Instructions:

1 . Melt the chocolate using a double boiler . Add in the water and gin and stir well .

2 . Heat until the mixture is very warm .

3 . Pour into a large mug . Top with whipped cream and sprinkle over the lime zest .

35) Naughty S ' Mores Hot Chocolate

Not your average campfire cocoa ! This cheeky hot chocolate is laced with whiskey and sweetened with honey .

Makes: 2

Preparation Time: 15mins

Ingredient List:

- 1 cup whole milk 1 cup heavy cream
- ½ cup semisweet choc chips 2 tablespoons runny honey
- 1 tablespoon simple sugar syrup
- ¼ cup chocolate syrup
- ¼ cup instant chocolate flavored pudding powder

2 ounces whiskey

ZZZZZZZZZZZZZZZZZZZZZZZZZZZZZZZZZZZZZZZZZZZZZZZZ
ZZZZZZZZZZZ

**Instructions
:**

1 . Into a saucepan over medium heat, add the milk and cream and warm together .

2 . In the meantime, melt the choc chips using a microwave .

3 . Add the melted chocolate to the milk / cream and add in the remaining ingredients .

4 . Whisk well and cook until heated through .

5 . Pour into mugs and serve .

Gingerbread Cookie Hot Chocolate

All the flavor of a gingerbread cookie with a big ole' kick of spiced rum .
What's not to love ! ?

Makes: 4
Preparation Time: 7mins
Ingredient List:

- 2 cups skim milk
- ½ cup milk choc chips
- ¼ cup molasses
- 1 tablespoon cocoa powder
- 1 teaspoon light brown sugar
- ½ teaspoons vanilla essence

- ½ teaspoons cinnamon
- ½ teaspoons fresh ginger (grated)
- ⅛ teaspoons
- nutmeg Pinch sea
- salt
- 4 ounces spiced rum

ZZZZZZZZZZZZZZZZZZZZZZZZZZZZZZZZZZZZZZZZZZZZZZ
ZZZZZZZZZZZ

Instructions
:

1 . Add all ingredients (excluding the rum) into a saucepan over med heat . Bring to a simmer for 5 minutes . Whisking continuously until the chocolate melts .

2 . Take off the heat and pour in the rum . Stir well .

3 . Pour into four mugs and serve !

37) Mudslide Chocolate

Is it a cocktail? Is it a hot chocolate? Is it both ! ? Who knows, but it ' s boozy and utterly delicious .

Makes: 4

Preparation Time: 15mins

Ingredient List:

- 2 cups whole milk
- ¼ cup granulated sugar
- 2 tablespoons cocoa powder 6 ounces milk choc chips
- 1 teaspoon vanilla essence
- ¼ cup Irish cream
- ¼ cup vodka

¼ cup coffee liqueur
Chocolate fudge sauce (for topping)
Whip cream (for topping)

ZZZZZZZZZZZZZZZZZZZZZZZZZZZZZZZZZZZZZZZZZZZZZZ
ZZZZZZZZZZ

Instructions
:
1 . Add the milk to a saucepan and simmer over medium heat .
2 . Add in the sugar and cocoa powder . Whisk until lump free .
3 . Toss in the choc chips and vanilla . Continue to cook until the chocolate has totally melted . Take off the heat and stir in the alcohols .
4 . Take tall glasses and drizzle chocolate fudge sauce all around the insides .
5 . Pour the hot chocolate into the dressed glasses and top with a dollop of whip cream .

38) Hot Chocolada

This hot chocolate pina colada hybrid will have you dream of warm summer breezes and tropical beaches .

Makes: 8
Preparation Time: 7mins
Ingredient List:

- 13½ ounces coconut milk
- 14 ounces sweetened condensed milk
- ½ cup unsweetened dark cocoa
- powder Pinch sea salt
- ¾ cup pineapple juice
- ¾ cup spiced
- rum 4 cups cold water

Instructions:

1 . Add the first 5 ingredients into a large saucepan and bring to a simmer . Take care not to boil . Whisk well and add the rum along with the cold water .

2 . Continue to heat until the hot chocolate is very warm .

3 . Pour into mugs and serve !

39) Mexican Eggnog Hot Chocolate

Nothing makes us feel more festive than a cup of hot chocolate or eggnog, so why not combine the two ! ?

Makes: 1

Preparation Time: 5mins

Ingredient List:

- 2 cups eggnog
- 1 sachet hot chocolate powder
- ⅛ teaspoons ground cinnamon
- ⅛ teaspoons ground nutmeg

ZZZZZZZZZZZZZZZZZZZZZZZZZZZZZZZZZZZZZZZZZZZZZZZZ
Instructions ZZZZZZZZZZZ
:

1 . Add the eggnog into a large mug and heat until steaming hot using the

microwave .

2 . Add in the hot chocolate powder and spices . Stir well until dissolved and serve !

40) Hot Chocolate with Irish Cream and Marshmallows

Nothing says fall or winter like toasted marshmallows ! This creamy, hot chocolate mix is the best way to beat the cold .

Makes:2 - 3
Preparation Time: 5mins
Ingredient List:

- 3 cups whole milk
- ⅓ cup half and half
- 1 cup semi - sweet chocolate chips
- ½ cup Irish Cream
- Mini marshmallows

ZZZZZZZZZZZZZZZZZZZZZZZZZZZZZZZZZZZZZZZZZZZZZZZ
Instructions ZZZZZZZZZZZ
:

1 . Using a small pan, and over medium heat, combine the milk with the half and half . Gently heat the liquid until steaming and add the chocolate chips.

2 . Whisk until the chocolate and milk have combined . Next, pour in the Irish Cream . Stir well to incorporate and pour into ovenproof mugs .

3 . Turn the broiler on low and place the mini marshmallows on top of the hot chocolate and put the mugs under the broiler . (Do not close the oven door).

4 . Watch carefully as the marshmallows will melt really fast . As soon as the marshmallows are toasty remove carefully from the heat, allow to cool a little and enjoy .

Printed in Great Britain
by Amazon

72064714R00052